IF YOU CAN DRAW THESE THINGS →
YOU WILL BE ABLE TO DRAW
ALL THE THINGS IN THIS BOOK.

△ ∧ S ⌣
□ ⊓ · | 〰
○ C D

FOR INSTANCE——

THE BOTTOM ROW TELLS WHAT TO DRAW. THE TOP ROW TELLS WHERE TO PUT IT.

HOPPER

BOXCAR

TANK CAR

PASSENGER CAR

STOCK CAR

LOG CARRIER

CABOOSE

OIL

STUFF

GONDOLA CAR

GRAIN CAR

FLAT CAR

EGGS

TROLLEY

COAL TENDER

OLD TRAIN

OLD PASSENGER CAR

DIESEL LOCOMOTIVE

MAIL

BAGGAGE CART

PASSENGERS

STATION

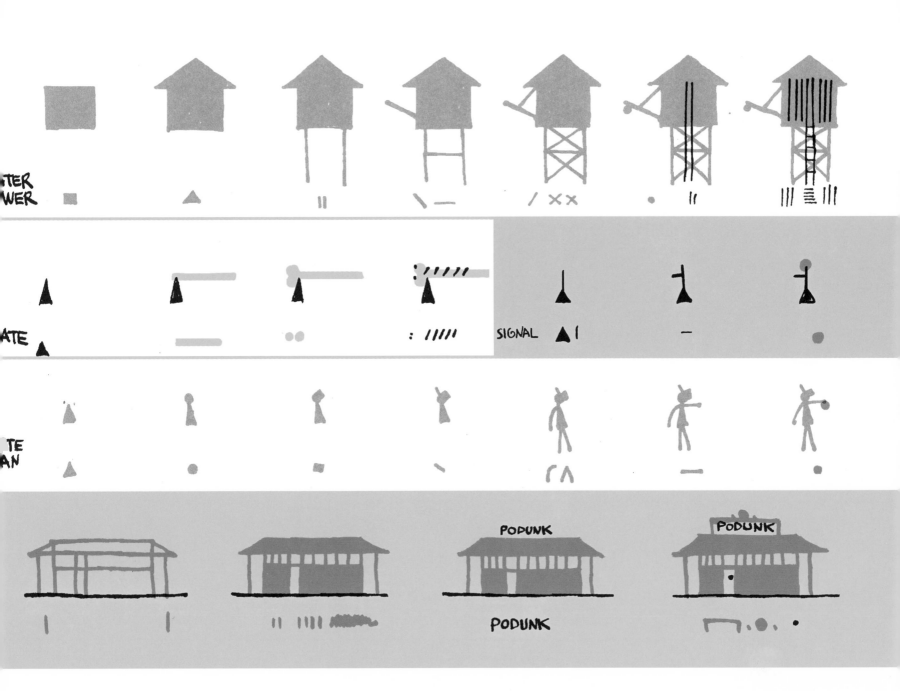

WATER
TOWER

GATE

GATE
MAN

SIGNAL

PODUNK

PODUNK

PODUNK

PICKUP TRUCKS

RADIO

ROLL BAR

TAILGATE

TAKES
SNOW PLOW
EXTENDED BODY

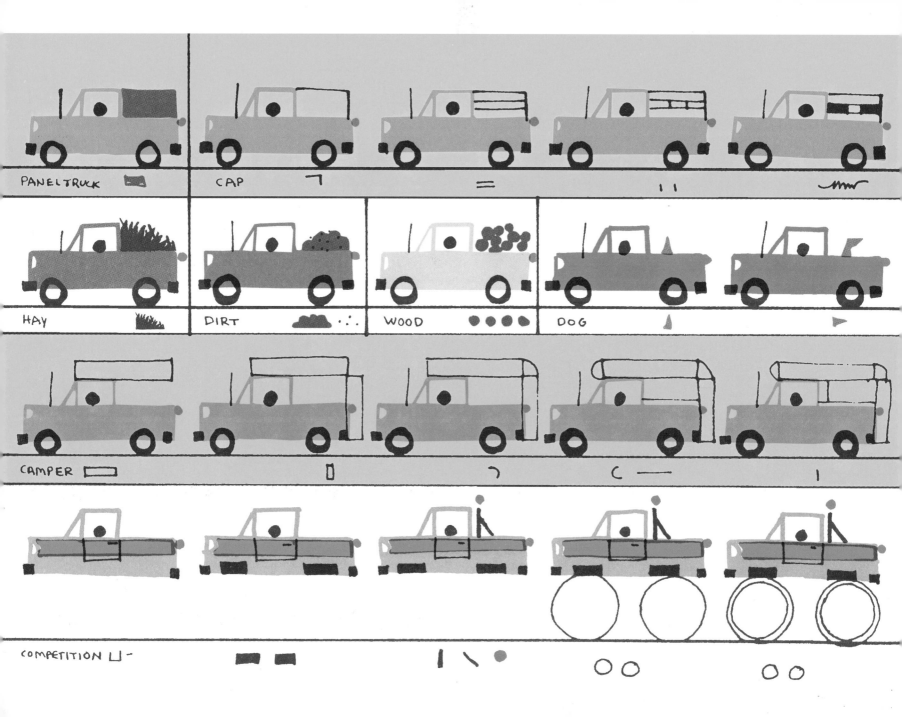

PANELTRUCK

CAP

HAY

DIRT

WOOD

DOG

CAMPER

COMPETITION

TOOL BOX

BIG TOOL BOX

LADDER

PIGS

VANS

PASSENGER VAN

FIX IT

FIX IT

FLOWERS

FLOWERS

STAND
UP

LONG BODY

HIGH ROOF

FISH

FISH

AMBULANCE

AMBULANCE

US MAIL

US MAIL

HEAVY TRUCKS

BED CAN BE SHORT → OR LONG → AND THIS FLATBED TRUCK CAN CARRY ALL SORTS OF THINGS

TOYS

ICE CREAM

ACME MOVERS

TOYS   ICE CREAM   ACME MOVERS

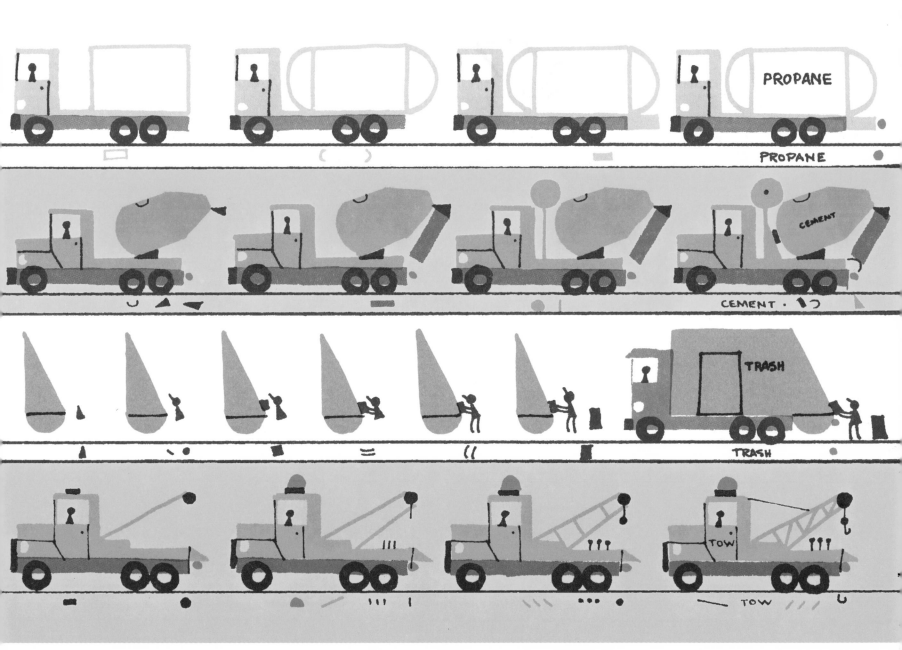

PROPANE

PROPANE

CEMENT

CEMENT

TRASH

TRASH

TOW

TOW

ADD TRUCK

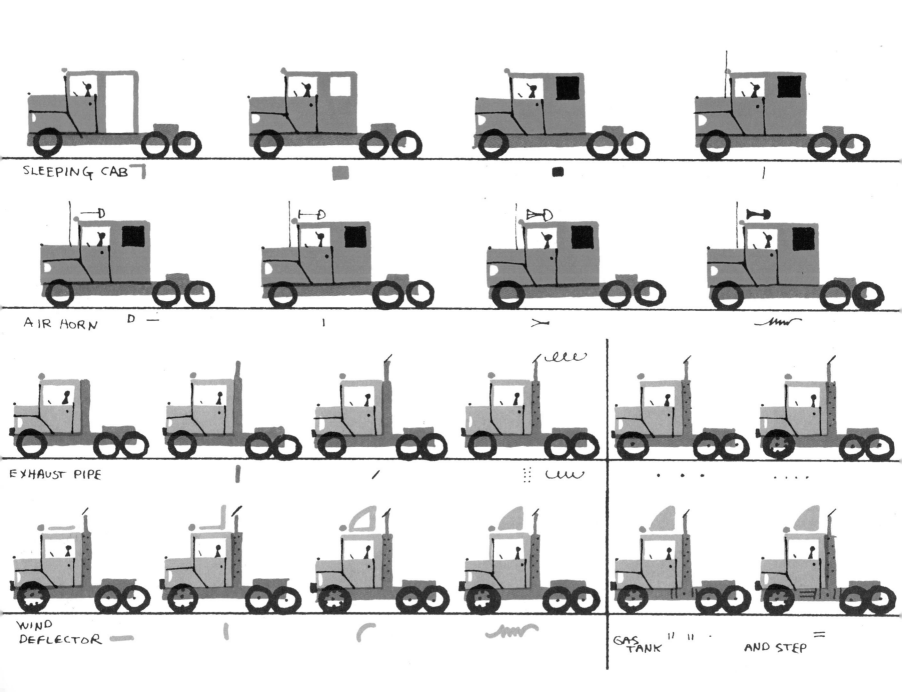

SLEEPING CAB

AIR HORN   D —

EXHAUST PIPE

WIND
DEFLECTOR —

GAS
TANK   AND STEP =

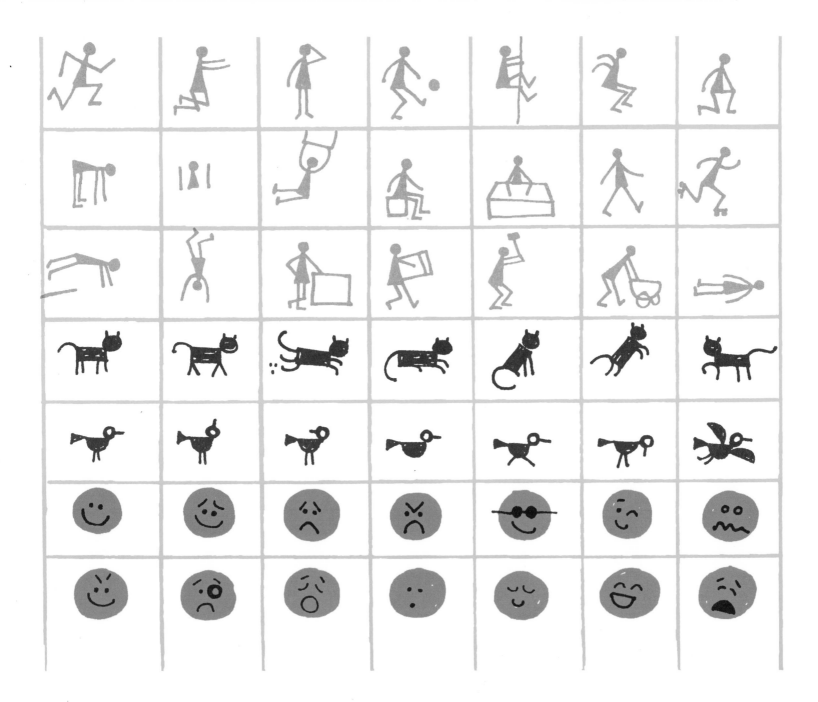

First Edition

ISBN 0-316-23898-8 (hc) / ISBN 0-316-23786-8 (pb)
LCCN 2001041744

10   9   8   7   6   5   4   3   2   1

TWP

Printed in Singapore